I dedicate this book to all the generous people who helped
and let me take these pictures; to my sons, Tonatiuh and Aidan,
for the adventures we shared while I worked on this project;
to Kieran for his support; to Horacio, Ireri and Elsa for their
enthusiasm; and to Gemma for her patience and understanding.

First published in Great Britain and in the USA in 2007
by Frances Lincoln Children's Books, 4 Torriano Mews,
Torriano Avenue, London NW5 2RZ

www.franceslincoln.com

British Library Cataloguing in Publication Data available on request

ISBN: 978-1-84507-593-4

Printed in Singapore

1 3 5 7 9 8 6 4 2

M is for Mexico

 Flor de María Cordero

FRANCES LINCOLN
CHILDREN'S BOOKS

Author's note

Mexico is a country with a wealth of cultures and friendly, vibrant people. Our main language is Spanish but nearly 60 other native languages are also spoken. Most people are Catholic but some rituals from our ancient cultures have made their way into our modern lives and some of our most famous food, like chocolate, has been adopted by countries throughout the world.

People living in Mexico sometimes have different opportunities depending on where they live or how rich they are. But they are always trying to find ways to improve their lives.

I am grateful to have the opportunity to tell you about the country where I was born – a country that always tries its hardest to keep its rich heritage, bright colours and delicious flavours alive.

Flor de Ma. Cordero

Aa

is for Alegría – a crunchy sweet treat made from toasted seeds mixed with honey and lemon juice. It is pressed into moulds to give it a round, rectangular or square shape. Alegría means happiness.

Bb

is for Baptism – the first religious ritual for babies. During the ceremony, the babies are named as they receive holy water and balm. After the ceremony, the Godparents throw coins to the crowd of attending children to wish for health and happiness for the baptised baby.

 **Cc** is for Chilli. Mexico has more varieties of chilli than any other country. This hot spice is used to flavour food – even chocolate and fruit. Ancient ceremonies to ask for good chilli crops are still held in some villages.

 **Dd**

is for Dancing. Sometimes people teach children to dance in public plazas or parks. They practise traditional and modern dances. You can find dancers every day in the streets, wearing colourful, eye-catching outfits with headdresses, feathers and rattles.

Ee

is for Escribano – a writer you can hire to type a letter or to fill out a form. These writers are established in public plazas with their typewriters. The highly skilled writers also produce documents that require beautiful handwriting.

Ff

is for Family. Mexican families can sometimes be very large. It is common to see parents and children building their homes in the same neighbourhood. Sunday lunch is a favourite time for a family to get together.

Gg

is for the Virgin of Guadalupe, Mexico's patron saint. The Basilica of Guadalupe was built to honour her. It is the largest church in the country and millions of people visit it every year to ask for miracles.

Hh

is for Huipil, a colourful dress worn by women and girls in some parts of Mexico. It is loose-fitting and brightly coloured. Sometimes the patterns show where the wearer is from and if she is married.

Ii

is for Insect. Grasshoppers, ants, insects or worms can be a pest, but in Mexico insects are cooked and eaten. Some insects can only be harvested at certain times of the year so they are a very expensive delicacy.

Jj

is for Jaguar, a big cat living in Mexico. The Mayans called it Balam, for it represented the God of Night. Aztec warriors used the jaguar as a symbol of force and courage. Today, the jaguars of Mexico are at risk from farming and building development which threaten their natural habitat.

 **Kk** is for Kitchen. Although many kitchens in Mexico have modern gadgets, some Mexicans still use older cooking methods. Traditional kitchens have stone grinders and wood-burning stoves made of clay.

Ll is for Lotería, the Mexican version of lotto. The boards have different pictures. The caller has the same pictures on cards. He shouts out each picture and the players mark the ones they have on their board. The caller will try to trick the players by chanting in rhymes or riddles. The winner is the first person to mark all the pictures on their board.

Mm

is for Mexico, a country with a diverse landscape – from tropical forests and deserts, to high mountains and coasts. It has big and beautiful cities whose people live fast-paced and modern lives, and little villages with people who keep the traditions of Mexico's ancient ancestors.

Nn

is for Nopal, a sour and slimy cactus. It is a very important ingredient in Mexican cooking, with a juicy and sweet fruit called tuna. A symbol of Mexico is an eagle eating a snake, perched on a nopal.

Oo

is for Organilleros. They play their tunes in public plazas, parks or streets. Each organ plays eight songs. The barrel organs were brought to Mexico from Europe more than 100 years ago.

is for Pyramid. These buildings were mainly temples or palaces. Some were built centuries before Christ was born. They were the central part of ancient cities. Some have been well-preserved and they are open to the public.

 is for Quinceañera, a fifteen-year-old girl. This is the age at which girls leave childhood behind. There is no birthday like this one! Wearing a beautiful dress, she attends mass and a party is given in her honour. She dances with a young man who she chooses.

Rr

is for Rituals. The Day of the Dead is one of Mexico's most important rituals. On the 1st and 2nd of November, Mexicans honour their loved ones who have died. Altars are set up in homes or at graves, with offerings of food. Relatives tidy up the graves, and bring fresh flowers and candles.

Ss is for School. In Mexico, children start school at the age of four. Some children who live in the countryside have lessons in one of the sixty native languages spoken in Mexico. In those schools, Spanish is taught as a second language.

Tt is for Tortilla, a soft flat bread made with corn dough. Usually they are eaten rolled and filled with savoury food. Then they are called tacos. Tortillas come in different sizes and colours, depending on the type of corn. In the cities, tortillas are made by huge machines, but some people still prefer to cook their own by hand.

Uu

is for Ulama, a ball game. It is
a very old sport first played by
warriors from Mexico's ancient
civilisations. The courts were built
next to temples. Ulama is played
with a rubber ball. The hips are used
to hit the ball and keep it in the air.

Vv

is for Voladores, men who honour the sun. Five voladores climb a pole at least 30 metres (100 feet) high. At the top, the leader dances to the north, south, east and west, and to the sun. Then four voladores each spin 13 times as they slowly descend. They make a total of 52 spins, the number of years in a century according to native calendars.

Ww

is for weavers. In Mexico, men and women weave baskets, blankets, rugs or hammocks. Natural fibres like cotton, silk and grass are often used in this beautiful tradition. They can be woven by hand or by using machines.

is for Xolo, a Mexican dog with
no hair, dark skin and pointy ears.
It has a very loyal character and
is an excellent guardian. A long time
ago it was believed this animal
helped human souls to reach the
Mictlan, a place like heaven. Xolo
is the short name for xoloitzcuintle,
pronounced *sho-low-eats-queen-tlay*.

is for Yunta – a pair of oxen, horses
or mules. Despite the use of tractors
and machinery for farming, these
animals are still used in some villages.
Once a year, people adorn their yuntas
with flowers and ribbons and parade
them through the town.

 **Zz** is for Zocalo, a main square or central plaza in a city. The zocalo is usually surrounded by the city hall, the cathedral and the market. Mexico City's zocalo is the third largest in the world, and every day there is something going on – a ceremony, a concert or a performance.